SUCCESSFULLY MASTERING JOB INTERVIEWS THROUGH 3-D STRATEGY

UNDERSTAND THE TRUE INTENTIONS BEHIND JOB INTERVIEW QUESTIONS. WORK OUT A PROPER, AUTHENTIC RESPONSE

ANTON C. HUBER

Copyright © Anton C. Huber
All Rights Reserved.

ISBN 978-1-63920-505-9

This book has been published with all efforts taken to make the material error-free after the consent of the author. However, the author and the publisher do not assume and hereby disclaim any liability to any party for any loss, damage, or disruption caused by errors or omissions, whether such errors or omissions result from negligence, accident, or any other cause.

While every effort has been made to avoid any mistake or omission, this publication is being sold on the condition and understanding that neither the author nor the publishers or printers would be liable in any manner to any person by reason of any mistake or omission in this publication or for any action taken or omitted to be taken or advice rendered or accepted on the basis of this work. For any defect in printing or binding the publishers will be liable only to replace the defective copy by another copy of this work then available.

Contents

Preface	v
Acknowledgements	vii
1. The Three Dimensions Of The 3-d-model	1
2. The First Dimension: 3 Basic Questions	3
3. The Second Dimension: 3 Time Levels	6
4. The Third Dimension: Authenticity	8
5. Questions In 30 Categories	10
6. Response Strategy In Job Interviews	34

Preface

Those who are invited for a job interview have already cleared the first hurdle. Based on the submitted documents the potential employer expects that the invitee is able to fill in the advertised position or in rare cases another position within the company.

In sports, one would say that the competitor has made it to the finals. Of often more than hundred applications, a handful is left, and the candidate is one of the chosen ones.

Whether the applicant masters the last challenges, so that it can come to a contract offer, now depends on several factors, which are the same everywhere. That is that the candidate deals with a professional personnel department. In this guide, I will cover these decisive factors. Thereby, I want to provide the reader with an advantage during the selection interview.

If you know what the interviewer expects from you, you will have a clear advantage.

I wish you a lot of success for your job interview.

Yours sincerely, Anton C. Huber

Senior Recruiting Specialist

Acknowledgements

In the series »to the point«, the publishers release short guides in a casual series, which have been written by a practitioner for practical use. »To the point« guides are limited to the most important information on an issue and reduce everything else to a minimum.

ONE
THE THREE DIMENSIONS OF THE 3-D-MODEL

The 3-D-model is based on the three basic dimensions of a job interview.

The first dimension includes the three basic questions, which a professional recruiter wants to clarify in every job interview. If only one of these three basic questions is not clarified satisfactorily, the candidate will not be considered further.

The second dimension, the dimension of the three levels of time, looks for an answer to the questions of where the candidate is mentally. Is he ready to tackle a new challenge? Or is he, for example, still in a phase where he tries to process the experiences from his last position?

The third dimension poses for many HR experts and candidates the biggest challenge. This dimension is about whether the answers of the candidate are authentic or just »learned well«.

SUCCESSFULLY MASTERING JOB INTERVIEWS THROUGH 3-D STRATEGY

A candidate has to be convincing on all three levels in order to »get to the next round« and, thus, to leave his competitors for the position behind.

TWO
THE FIRST DIMENSION: 3 BASIC QUESTIONS

In the year 2011, George Bradt headed his article in Forbes with the title: »Top executive recruiters agree there are only three true job interview questions.«

In fact, he revealed nothing new with that but rather outlined a fact that is long familiar to every HR department, that has earned its reputation. Job interviews are about clarifying the questions concerning skills and motivation and, eventually, it should become apparent whether the candidate fits into the company, into the department, and into the team.

Candidates can gain a significant advantage by also considering the tree dimensions with the questions, as far as it is relevant. A classic question, which provides you with many opportunities hereto, is the well-known »why you« question.

»Can you do the job?« - skills

SUCCESSFULLY MASTERING JOB INTERVIEWS THROUGH 3-D STRATEGY

The question of skills is probably the simplest. If the employer did not assume that you have the necessary skills for the job, he would not have invited you. This is mainly about verifying that the information in your resume and the other documents is truly accurate. Moreover, information, which is not apparent from the documents, is added.

Also, an important aspect is to show your own skills in this context. It makes a difference whether a result, so to say, fell to you or whether you achieved it through active influence.

»Will you love the job?« - Motivation

No employer will hire employees, who only apply for the position to have »at least something«. As an internal (or external) service provider, he has to get the impression that you really want the position.

You can score if you can show that you have already, in advance, dealt with the position and the potential employer, in this category of questions

Promising approaches are:

- You show that you have already acquainted yourself with the company, their products, their position and the market environment with your own questions, but also with your answers.
- You indicate that you already identify emotionally with the advertised position by using phrases, such as: »in the advertised position I could ...«. But also, be careful with statements that could give the interviewer the impression that you already had the position. Your interlocutor could then feel ignored and could react accordingly negatively.

- Show interest in your future position. It may be appropriate to ask about a typical day in the job etc.

An important advantage in every application process may be if you, as far as this possibility exists, have already gotten in contact with the person that was mentioned in the advertised position or with an acquaintance that works in said company. This way, you might get some answers to important questions in advance, so that you, in turn, are able to show a specific interest in the company during the job interview.

»Can we tolerate working with you?« - Does it fit?

The best qualifications and the convincing motivation of a candidate are useless if the he does not fit into the team. This question is admittedly the most difficult. You probably do not know the team and the company only from the outside. From your perspective, you will hardly be able to do more than show interest (preparation, have questions, etc.)

THREE

THE SECOND DIMENSION: 3 TIME LEVELS

Within the second dimension, of the 3 time levels, primarily one answer to the question of whether you are emotionally ready to accept a new challenge, is wanted.

Those who endlessly refer to previous positions with their answers will give the impression that they have not yet emotionally cut the cord from their last position and will be a risk for the new employer.

Even a socially minded manager, who tries to support his employees, will not want to hire someone that needs support from a coach or a psychologist in order to put their last position behind. It is also counterproductive to give lectures on how it was »previously with company X« in every discussion.

An optimal distribution for respective answers is: 20% past, 40% presence, and 40% future expectations. That means that you can start with experiences from the past, but it is advisable to lay stress on what is today and in the future. A simplified example may be: »I have experienced X, from that I have learned Y for my life and helps me to seek Z in the future.«

FOUR

THE THIRD DIMENSION: AUTHENTICITY

Do you know guides on the topic: »What do I say when I am asked for weaknesses«? How can I elaborate on weaknesses which my interlocutor sees as strengths? A frequently mentioned option here is »impatience«.

Hundreds of candidates respond with that. If you sat »on the other side of the table« and heard the answer for the umpteenth time, you would probably feel ridiculed.

Nothing can be said against the response »impatience«, if it corresponds to the truth. It is much more important for the interviewer whether you are authentic than the actual answers to this and other questions. Overall, it can make sense draw a link from weaknesses t positive aspects if there are any, or, for example, to refer what you do in order to work on your weakness.

Your interlocutor wants to perceive you as an honest person whose answers also correspond to the reality. Answers that come across as well prepared and memorized have a dissuasive effect on the other person. Such answers have already spoilt it for many candidates that sat facing me.

A recruiter cannot risk suggesting an imposter to his (internal or external) customers, who does not deliver what he promises. For this reason, people, who do not seem authentic, are immediately sorted out by me and most of my colleagues.

FIVE

Questions in 30 Categories

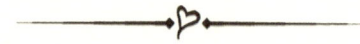

The following 30 questions show the most frequently asked questions in a job interview and are sorted by the questions that the interviewer wants to ask you. In every questions category, you can also find the desired qualifications, which your interlocutor wants to clarify the question.

Do not make the mistake to learn the questions and answers by heart. Think of the third dimension, credibility! It can, however, make sense to already give various questions a few thoughts in advance, and especially, to briefly analyze what information the other person wants to get from the question. This helps you to come »to the point« quicker.

Active listening

- How do you make sure that you have understood the other person correctly?
- Explain a particularly momentous misunderstanding from your professional past.

- Has is happened before that colleague turned to you for advice for non-job-related issues? How did you react?
- How do you proceed when you have the impression that you have not understood the other person correctly?
- How do you proceed when you are involved in a conflict?

Qualifications:

- Is a good listener.
- Successfully applies deescalating discussion techniques.
- Tries to understand his interlocutor.
- Avoid hasty judgments.
- Is an esteemed interlocutor of his colleagues.

Appearance

- How do you come across to other people? Have you already received feedback from your professional environment? What feedback?
- What bothers you the most when you appear in public?
- How do you feel before an important professional meeting? How do you prepare for it?
- How do your business partners react to you? How do you explain that?
- Describe a situation where a public appearance did not proceed optimally for you. What were the reasons?

Qualifications:

- Presents himself confidently and determined in foreign environments.
- Realistically estimates his effect on his environment.
- Has an authentic appearance.
- Has good manners that are well-adapted to the situation.
- Has a positive attitude.

Endurance

- What determines whether you follow through with a once made decision?
- Under what circumstances do you come back to a once made decision?
- How do you deal with routine work? Give an example.
- What type of tasks gives you energy, which cost you particularly much energy?
- Describe a situation where you did not achieve a result despite great efforts.
- How important is it to you to bring constant output and how do you manage that?
- Have you already dealt with resistance during your professional career? Name an example and explain how you handled it.
- Is perseverance an important property in your eyes? How does this show in your professional career?
- If you have started one thing, under what conditions do you bring this to an end?
- In which situations in your professional career have you given up to early?

Qualifications:

- Pursues goals consistently.

- Has perseverance.
- Brings started tasks to an end.
- Maintains performance level and overview even under time pressure.
- Can also handle resistances.

Resistance

- Explain a situation where you felt under pressure. How did you proceed and what was the result?
- How do you react when someone gives you a bigger, urgent job shortly before finishing time or weekend?
- Describe a work situation in which you felt overloaded.
- How do you react to disruptions and disturbances in your work?
- Describe a situation in which you had to overcome some obstacles in order to achieve your goal.

Qualifications:

- Possesses stress resistance.
- Is friendly and humorous.
- Displays willingness to take on additional tasks.
- Confidently deals with disturbances.
- Displays readiness for extra tasks.
- Preserves peace and overview in hectic situations.
- Does not even give up when difficulties and resistances come up.
- Displays minor performance fluctuations.
- Has burnout resistance.

Empathy

- How do you recognize what is important to your interlocutor?
- How do you adjust yourself to business partners/employees? - Give a concrete example.
- What has been the most difficult person you had to get along with? How did you proceed? What was the result?
- How do you proceed when you have the impression that one colleague does not feel good at the moment?

Qualifications:

- Can adjust to the needs of his interlocutor.
- Recognizes the state of the person opposite from him and can adjust to that.
- Has considerations for the feelings and need of others.
- Recognizes interpersonal conflicts and reacts appropriately.

Willingness to make decisions

- What decisions do your prefer to avoid?
- What leeway in decision-making did you have in your previous career and what would you have needed in order to achieve (even) better results?
- Do you ensure yourself when you make a decision? How? How have your experiences been with that?
- How do you proceed when you need to make important decisions?
- Do you ask others for advice when you have to make a decision? How do you deal with advice if you consider it wrong?
- Describe a decision and its consequences which were particularly positive in retrospect.

- How could you improve your decision-making ability?
- Describe a decision which you made too late, from today's perspective, or where you decided wrongly. What would you do differently from today's perspective?
- Based on what criteria do you make decisions?
- Where do you have an easy time making decisions and where do you find it hard?
- What are your particular strengths in decision-making?
- Has it already happened that you have changed decisions after it had been criticized? Give an example.

Qualifications:

- Decides on time.
- Decides deliberately.
- Considers advice of professionals for decisions.
- Uses leeway in decision-making.

Expertise

- How did you acquire your expertise and how do you keep it up to date?
- How successful were you compared to your colleagues (in your job, studies, apprenticeship)
- Have you received special recognition for your professional skills in the past? From whom and for what?
- What role does your expertise play for your professional success?

Qualifications:

- Is a recognized expert on his territory.

- Finds his way in his field of expertise.
- Has a wide experience base.
- Has a good overview of his field of expertise.

Flexibility

- Describe a situation in your professional context in which you had to change your planned practice spontaneously? What was the reason? How did you proceed? What was the result?
- Under what conditions are you most efficient?
- How do you handle new situations and challenges?
- What change has been the biggest challenge for you in your professional past? How did you cope with it?
- How do you rate your own openness towards new conditions?
- How do you handle colleagues in a team or a project who come from different cultures or countries? Give an example.

Qualifications:

- Ability to work in diverse teams.
- Take up suggestions from others.
- Tolerates other and their (different) opinion.
- Adapts to the situation concerning working hours.
- Can adapt to new situations and people.
- Can cope with disturbances and challenging situations.

Frustration tolerance

- Tell us about your last professional failure. How did you manage it?

- How do you motivate yourself after a failure?
- How do handle it if you do not feel supported by colleagues?
- Describe a serious personal setback in your professional past.
- What discourages you?
- How do you handle rejection?
- Describe a situation in which you wanted to quit your job.
- What did you find particularly frustrating in your past job?
- How do you handle not having success despite great personal efforts?
- What makes you angry?
- How do you deal with the situation when you need data or documents for your work, but you do not receive it from the respective colleague?
- Are you rather optimistic or pessimistic compared to your former colleagues?
- How do you react when other people discomfit you?

Qualifications:

- Is not discouraged by failures.
- Finishes necessary thing even if they are not fun.
- Can motivate himself.
- Does not show frustration to others.
- Handles setback constructively.
- Does not feel personally attacked in controversial discussions.

Initiative

- Has there been a situation in your (professional) past where you took charge of something and realized it successfully? What was the result?
- How do you win new customers? Describe a specific case from your past. (This question can also be posed to employees without a direct selling order.)
- Did you propose innovations or improvements in your last position? Have these been implemented? (Why/why not?)
- Describe a situation in which recognized a good business opportunity. How did you handle it?

Qualifications:

- Willingness to also participate in fields outside his own core competency.
- Existing innovation ability/willingness.
- Takes initiative.
- Develops ideas of one's own accord.
- Is not satisfied with what he achieved, but look for ways to improve.
- Focused on the client.
- Has ideas for client acquisition and its implementation.
- Makes successful suggestions for improvement.
- Makes constructive and expedient suggestions for improvement.

Integrity

- How do you handle it when goals and requirements of your job interfere with your own? Give an example.
- How do you deal with it when you have problems with a person (boss, colleague, subordinate) in your

environment?
- There are situations where your task may require you to do something that you would not normally do or what is contrary to your values. Were there such situations in your professional past? How did you handle them?

Qualifications:

- Seems upright and trustworthy.
- Behavior and values match.
- Can differentiate between personal and professional necessities.
- Supports enterprise policy unreservedly against the outside.
- Moves within legal regulations and ethical norms.
- Implements required action.

Integration ability / integration willingness

- How do you proceed when you come into a new team as the new person?
- How do you proceed when new colleagues enter your team?
- How do you handle dissent and different ideas?
- Have you already worked in teams with people from different cultural backgrounds in the past? What was your experience with it?
- How do you succeed to fascinate other people for common goals?
- Do you succeed more when you work alone or in a team?

Qualifications:

- Can easily integrate himself into a team.
- Can integrate other employees into a team.
- Can easily integrate himself into heterogeneous/intercultural teams.
- Achieves results nicely in a team.
- Imparts goals and values to others.

Creativity

- What role does creativity play in your profession?
- What specific changes and improvements have you introduced in previous positions, or with which changes and improvements did you take part in introducing them?
- What has been your most original idea up to now? How did you realize it?
- How do you proceed when you have an idea on how to improve something work-related? Describe a specific event from your professional record. What were the results?

Qualifications:

- Successfully goes new ways.
- Is able to develop creative solutions and also implement them.
- Stimulates innovations through his ideas.
- Thinks and also finds unconventional solutions.

Conflict behavior

- How do you behave in a conflict?
- What conflicts do you prefer to avoid?

- What do you do to resolve a conflict?
- What has been the biggest conflict up to now which you experienced within a work context and how did you solve it?
- When do conflicts represent chances for you?

Qualifications:

- Can handle conflicts constructively.
- Can also implement measures when they are unpopular and entail the risk of conflict.
- Deals with conflicts in a competent way.
- Does not avoid conflicts.

Ability to establish conflicts and appearance

- How do you usually get in contact with new colleagues, customers or strangers?
- What does networking mean to you? Which experiences did you have with it?
- How to you proceed when you have to integrate into a team?
- Are you a team player?
- Describe a situation in which the interaction with customers was particularly positive. What could you have done to achieve even better results in the situation?
- How often do you go out with colleagues outside working hours?
- How important is it to you to be together with others?
- How important is a positive interaction with your colleagues to you?

Qualifications:

- Can easily make contact with others.
- Actively approaches other people.
- Can easily win others over.
- Easily integrates into an existing team.
- Has a good relationship with his business partners.
- Has a positive attitude towards people.

Commitments

- What performance from your past makes your particularly proud? Why?
- What are usually your goals that you set for yourself?
- What motivates you to deliver top performance?
- What do you demand from yourself and other when they begin with a task? Give examples.
- Talk about a situation in which you »outgrew yourself« and, thus, achieved particular success.

Qualifications:

- Has above-average motivation.
- Is enthusiastic for tasks.
- Displays punctuality.
- Displays willingness to go the »extra mile«.
- Demands a lot from himself and others.
- Sees tasks as opportunities for improvement.

Willingness to learn

- How do you improve yourself (outside of work)?
- How do you keep your expertise up to date?
- How many hours per month do you use to improve and educate yourself further?

- What was the last reference book from your field of expertise that you have read last? Why this one?
- In which phase of your professional career have you worked particularly hard on yourself? How?
- What changes in your field of expertise are pending at the moment and how do you prepare for them?

Qualifications:

- Keeps knowledge up to date.
- Has motivation to improve himself.
- Willingness and ability to educate himself further.
- Has knowledge in related fields.
- Self-motivation for training/improvement is available.

Leadership of employees

- How do you decide which tasks you delegate to which employee?
- How do you delegate the tasks to employees?
- How do you ensure that the employees attend to their delegated tasks on time and in good quality?
- How do you proceed when an employee does not work on a delegated task to your satisfaction?
- How do you encourage employees?
- What was your most difficult situation with an employee up to now? How did you solve this?
- What influence do employees have on your decision-making?
- How do you ensure that your employees know what you expect from them?
- How do you ensure that your employees know how you evaluate their performance?

- What are your particular strengths in encouraging and promoting others?
- Have you ever received feedback on your leadership from subordinates? Which feedback? Describe the reason.

Qualification:

- Is an experienced leader.
- Is accepted as a leader by the employees.
- Agrees with employees on their goals and controls these.
- Delegates tasks according to skills.
- Gives regular feedback to the employees.
- Encourages the employees in their development.

Motivation (depends on position)

- In what part of the task are you most interested?
- Why did you apply for especially this position?
- Why did you choose this profession?
- What motivates you most (in work context)?

Qualifications:

- Identifies with the work.
- Sees work as a challenge.
- Completes work quickly and thoroughly.
- Shows commitment to his tasks even outside work hours.
- Has fun at work.

Oral wording

- What are your strengths in communication?
- Have you ever received feedback on your ability to present issues? Which feedback?
- In what area would you like to improve your ability to present?
- When was the last time you gave a presentation in front of strangers/acquaintances? Describe your success and how you felt during the presentation?
- How do you prepare for a presentation?
- Do you find it easy to explain complex issues to people, so that they are able to understand them?
- Do you prefer to communicate via telephone or via email? Why? What are the advantages and disadvantages?
- How big was the biggest audience (number) in front of which you had to make a speech / give a presentation? How did you feel before / while doing it?
- Has there been a situation where you were misunderstood in a presentation? What was the reason? What were the consequences?

Qualifications:

- Presents issues clearly, understandable and in a structured way.
- Is eloquent.
- Speaks in a structured and understandable way.
- Speaks fluently and in a differentiated way.
- Prepares presentations effectively.
- Is able to give a presentation in front of a large crowd.

Implementation skills

- If you have made a decision, how do you proceed to implement it?
- The implementation of what decisions do you find particularly difficult? Why?
- How do you proceed when you must implement a decision of which you are not convinced?
- How do you proceed to convince your team of a common goal and how do you encourage it to achieve this goal together?
- Imagine, I was your customer. Explain the advantages of the main product of your previous employer to me in contrast to the product of the competition.
- What makes it particularly difficult for your to implement a decision? Describe a respective situation from your professional past.

Qualifications:

- Is able to implement decisions.
- Conveys common goals and values to others.
- Positively influences team building.
- Can enthuse himself and others for something.
- Achieves goals together with others.
- Is able to also implement tasks that he thinks of as critical.
- Works systematically and goal-oriented.
- Includes his whole team to achieve a goal.

Judgment

- How do you proceed when you have to make a decision?
- Do you sometimes experience sleepless nights before an important decision?

- Which was the single most important decision in your life up to now? How did you proceed? How do you value your decision in hindsight?
- Which was the single most difficult decision in your life up to now? How did you proceed? How do you value your decision in hindsight?

Qualifications:

- Is responsible with decisions.
- Detects problems and realistically estimates their causes and effects.
- Makes decisions deliberately.
- Considers information from different sources as a basis for decisions.

Planning and organization

- Were you able to succeed through good planning in the past? Please tell us about it.
- How do you proceed when you take over a new field?
- How do you ensure that you solve your tasks successfully?
- How do you keep track of your unfinished work?
- What do you do to work even more efficiently?
- How do you plan your work day?

Qualifications:

- Sets clear priorities.
- Knows what is important.
- Adheres to deadlines and cost regulations.
- Has his tasks under control.

- Works systematically.
- Sets clear goals and pursues them consistently.
- Is a thorough planner.

Problem analysis

- How do you proceed when you have to solve a problem?
- With the help of which method do you prioritize your daily tasks?
- What role does intuition play when solving problems?
- Explain how you approached a task and what results you have achieved by reference to a concrete problem.
- What type of problems provides the greatest challenge for you? How do you handle it?
- Describe a problem from your professional life which you were unable to solve despite full effort. How did you proceed? Why were you not successful?
- What was the most difficult problem you had to solve until now? How did you proceed?

Qualifications:

- Thinks analytically in processes and structures.
- Realistically assesses tasks.
- Views problems as challenges.
- Quickly conceives problems and perceives overall contexts.
- Actively obtains missing information.
- Quickly gets an overview and is able to set intermediate goals and priorities.
- Obtains missing information.

Written mode of expression

- Have you ever written texts that was dedicated to several persons (e.g. customers, several employees, business partners)? What feedback did you get?
- What was the most demanding text you have ever written and what results did you achieve with it?
- Have you ever written something that was intended for a broader audience (publication in a magazine, newspaper, the internet, a book)? What were the feedbacks like?
- How would you proceed if you had t write an article on the topic ... for a magazine? How would you start? How would you structure the article? How do you feel during the process?

Qualifications:

- Has experience in writing texts for a wider audience.
- Is able to present issues comprehensibly and clearly.
- Writes concisely.
- Expresses himself clearly and comprehensibly.
- Is also able to manage and structure bigger writing tasks.

Self-sufficiency

- What responsibilities in you last job did you perform independently? On what tasks did you have to consult others?
- Were the situations in the past where you had to make decisions without being able to consult someone even though you were supposed to? What consequences did arise?

- Were there situations where you felt left alone by supervisors? How did you handle such situation?
- Does it happen that colleagues ask you for your advice? Give an example.

Qualifications:

- Also holds opinions against pushback.
- Works autonomously to targets.
- Solves problems without delegation and permanent hedge.
- Is willing to make decisions and stand behind them if necessary.
- Know how to help himself in a challenging situation.

Diligence

- Describe a mistake that you have made during a previous job which had serious impacts. What have you learned from it?
- During what tasks during your past job was thorough work particularly important? How did you solve this task?
- How do you proceed in order to make as few mistakes at work as possible?
- What mistakes during work could be eliminated due to your suggestions or activities?
- How do you handle it if you have made a mistake?

Qualifications:

- Works accurately and thoroughly.
- Also considers details.

- Precisely sticks to specifications.
- Optimizes himself.
- Is reliable and trustworthy.

Ability to work in a team

- How important is teamwork for you?
- Have you had challenging situations when working in a team during your professional past? Which and how did you manage them?
- What role do you assume in a team?
- How do you work in a team? Give examples.

Qualifications:

- Is a successful team player.
- Works together with a group in order to achieve a shared goal.
- Is appreciated by colleagues.
- Is also oriented on targets outside his own field.
- Includes colleagues and achieves shared added values.
- Adapts to the individual group members.

Negotiation skills

- How are you at enforcing your negotiation goal in a negotiation? Describe a concrete example from your job.
- What has been your best idea to win somebody over until now?
- What is your biggest challenge during negotiations? How do you manage this? Give a concrete example.
- How do you prepare for an important negotiation?

- Have there been cases where you did not achieve your goals in negotiations? What would you do differently in a similar case?

Qualifications:

- Can enforce himself and his goals in a negotiation.
- Achieves his goals without being too dominant.
- Considers arguments of interlocutors and responds to them.
- Argues clearly and conclusively.
- Knows how to help himself.
- Specifically prepares for negotiations.

Ability to sell

- How do you prepare for a customer meeting?
- What has been your greatest sales success? How did you proceed with that? Is there anything that you could have done even better from today's perspective?
- Describe how you explain a complex issue to a layman. Give an example.
- What has been your greatest sales failure? What have you learned from it?
- How do you handle conflicts? Give a concrete example from a situation with a customer.
- What conflicts do you prefer to avoid?
- What about selling gives you the greatest joy?
- Do you find approaching new customers easy? Describe an experience where you succeeded specifically.

- What do you think is the decisive factor for someone deciding for your offer?
- In what situations do you find it particularly hard to sell products/services?

Qualifications:

- Finds the right tone.
- Can argue geared to a target group.
- Skillfully achieves his conversation goal.
- Can be enthusiastic about a matter.
- Prepares well.
- Is good in selling.
- Reacts to customer concerns.
- Is able to influence critical situations positively.

SIX

RESPONSE STRATEGY IN JOB INTERVIEWS

Especially during interview situations it can happen that people reveal more about themselves than they really wanted to or than is good for them.

The risk is particularly high when a candidate »feels safe« and relaxed after a stressful situation. Many then start to chat. Aside from the fact that one then easily loses control over what he says, alone the mere fact that one gives up the control can help the other person to draw certain conclusions about the suitability of a particular person.

You will respond best if you briefly think about what the interlocutor wants to find out by asking the question. This way, your answers will come across best. Also, try to include your knowledge about the three dimensions and, thus, provide the other person with arguments that will bring you into the »next round«.

In any case, brace yourself for surprising questions as well as for usual questions about your resume, strengths, weaknesses, etc.

www.ingramcontent.com/pod-product-compliance
Lightning Source LLC
Chambersburg PA
CBHW020713180526
45163CB00008B/3068